All Rights Reserved
© Kari Denker 2018

Welcome!

This Biblical Meditation Series is designed to help you meditate through the entire Bible in about three years. The series will help you read through each chapter of the Bible at a pace that allows you to meditate, apply, pray, and enjoy your time in the Word. At the end of the series, you will have created your own personal commentary of your time spent in the Bible.

The series continues with Volume Two. In this volume we will finish reading Exodus then move on to Mark, then Leviticus, then finish with Luke. Each volume will take you through approximately a quarter of a year but can be started at any time.

Each day you work in this book, you will read the chapter (or short chapters) written at the top of the page, then you'll fill in each of the boxes on the two-page spread for that day. There is a page for each Monday through Saturday for you to work in, and on Sunday there are two pages for reflection on the previous week's work.

My hope and prayer is that as you work through these pages you'll have time to slow down and think deeply about the truth in the Bible and how it applies to your life and your growth as His child.

Find out more at: www.stonesoupforfive.com or join a group of people working through this together on Facebook at:
www.facebook.com/StoneSoupForFive.

☐ pray before beginning

Exodus 13

Date:

Summarize the main idea(s) in this chapter:

Verse(s) that stood out   or   **Who is in this chapter? What do they say? What do they do?**

Why did I pick this verse?   or   **What is going on? Is there anything going wrong?**

Definitions of words and/or cross references from my verse   or   **When and where did this happen?**

#Iwillmeditate

Rewrite the verse in your own words   or   Why is this chapter in the Bible?
or personalize it.   Why did these events happen?
                                                                                  Why did the people act this way?

Does this verse reveal anything about God/Jesus/Holy Spirit?
Are there examples to follow or avoid?   What does this chapter have to teach me?

How can I apply insights from this verse today? This week?

Notes, quotes, doodles, checklists, prayers, etc.

#Iwillmeditate

☐ pray before beginning

Exodus 14

Date:

Summarize the main idea(s) in this chapter:

Verse(s) that stood out or **Who is in this chapter? What do they say? What do they do?**

Why did I pick this verse? or **What is going on? Is there anything going wrong?**

Definitions of words and/or cross references from my verse or **When and where did this happen?**

#Iwillmeditate

Rewrite the verse in your own words   or   Why is this chapter in the Bible?
or personalize it.   Why did these events happen?
                                            Why did the people act this way?

Does this verse reveal anything about God/Jesus/Holy Spirit?
Are there examples to follow or avoid? What does this chapter have to teach me?

How can I apply insights from this verse today? This week?

Notes, quotes, doodles, checklists, prayers, etc.

#Iwillmeditate

☐ pray before beginning

Exodus 15

Date:

Summarize the main idea(s) in this chapter:

Verse(s) that stood out   or   Who is in this chapter?
                                              What do they say? What do they do?

Why did I pick this verse?   or   What is going on?
                                              Is there anything going wrong?

Definitions of words and/or   or   When and where
cross references from my verse   did this happen?

#Iwillmeditate

Rewrite the verse in your own words   or   Why is this chapter in the Bible?
or personalize it.   Why did these events happen?
                                                                         Why did the people act this way?

Does this verse reveal anything about God/Jesus/Holy Spirit?
Are there examples to follow or avoid? What does this chapter have to teach me?

How can I apply insights from this verse today? This week?

Notes, quotes, doodles, checklists, prayers, etc.

#Iwillmeditate

☐ pray before beginning

Exodus 16

Date:

Summarize the main idea(s) in this chapter:

Verse(s) that stood out   or   Who is in this chapter? What do they say? What do they do?

Why did I pick this verse?   or   What is going on? Is there anything going wrong?

Definitions of words and/or cross references from my verse   or   When and where did this happen?

#Iwillmeditate

Rewrite the verse in your own words or Why is this chapter in the Bible?
or personalize it. Why did these events happen?
Why did the people act this way?

Does this verse reveal anything about God/Jesus/Holy Spirit?
Are there examples to follow or avoid? What does this chapter have to teach me?

How can I apply insights from this verse today? This week?

Notes, quotes, doodles, checklists, prayers, etc.

#Iwillmeditate

☐ pray before beginning

Exodus 17-18

Date:

Summarize the main idea(s) in this chapter:

Verse(s) that stood out or **Who is in this chapter? What do they say? What do they do?**

Why did I pick this verse? or **What is going on? Is there anything going wrong?**

Definitions of words and/or cross references from my verse or **When and where did this happen?**

#Iwillmeditate

Rewrite the verse in your own words   or   Why is this chapter in the Bible?
or personalize it.   Why did these events happen?
                                                                                  Why did the people act this way?

Does this verse reveal anything about God/Jesus/Holy Spirit?
Are there examples to follow or avoid? What does this chapter have to teach me?

How can I apply insights from this verse today? This week?

Notes, quotes, doodles, checklists, prayers, etc.

#Iwillmeditate

☐ pray before beginning

Exodus 19-20

Date:

Summarize the main idea(s) in this chapter:

Verse(s) that stood out   or   **Who is in this chapter? What do they say? What do they do?**

Why did I pick this verse?   or   **What is going on? Is there anything going wrong?**

Definitions of words and/or cross references from my verse   or   **When and where did this happen?**

#Iwillmeditate

Rewrite the verse in your own words   or   Why is this chapter in the Bible?
or personalize it.   Why did these events happen?
                                              Why did the people act this way?

Does this verse reveal anything about God/Jesus/Holy Spirit?
Are there examples to follow or avoid? What does this chapter have to teach me?

How can I apply insights from this verse today? This week?

Notes, quotes, doodles, checklists, prayers, etc.

#Iwillmeditate

☐ pray before beginning

Review and reflect #14

Date:

Review each of the last six days work. Write or list the main takeaway you got from each chapter. (Look closely at the sections "What does this reveal about God?" and "How can I apply this?")

Are there any themes showing up in this week's work?

Are there any areas God is wanting to grow my faith or trust?
Are there any insights from this week's work on how to do this?

Are there any sins God is spotlighting in my life?
Are there any insights from this week's work on how to kill these sins?

#Iwillmeditate

Re-read one or two of the most impactful verses from this week and turn them into a prayer. (There is room on the next pages to write it down if you want.)

How can I thank or praise God as a result of what I've learned this week?

How can I apply what I've learned this week to my life today and next week?

Where do I need His strength for today? Tomorrow? Next week?

Is there a verse from this week that I should commit to memory? Write it on the next page or on a 3x5 card to take with you to memorize.

Are there any sins I need to confess to God in prayer?

Is there anyone I need to forgive? Is there anyone I need to ask forgiveness of?

Are there any seeds of bitterness starting to take root in my heart?

Are there any fears or worries I need to lay at His feet?

notes, verses to memorize

prayers, doodles, etc

☐ pray before beginning

Exodus 21

Date:

Summarize the main idea(s) in this chapter:

Verse(s) that stood out   or   Who is in this chapter?
What do they say? What do they do?

Why did I pick this verse?   or   What is going on?
Is there anything going wrong?

Definitions of words and/or   or   When and where
cross references from my verse   did this happen?

#Iwillmeditate

Rewrite the verse in your own words or personalize it.

or

Why is this chapter in the Bible?
Why did these events happen?
Why did the people act this way?

Does this verse reveal anything about God/Jesus/Holy Spirit?
Are there examples to follow or avoid? What does this chapter have to teach me?

How can I apply insights from this verse today? This week?

Notes, quotes, doodles, checklists, prayers, etc.

#Iwillmeditate

☐ pray before beginning

Exodus 22

Date:

Summarize the main idea(s) in this chapter:

Verse(s) that stood out   or   Who is in this chapter? What do they say? What do they do?

Why did I pick this verse?   or   What is going on? Is there anything going wrong?

Definitions of words and/or cross references from my verse   or   When and where did this happen?

#Iwillmeditate

Rewrite the verse in your own words or personalize it.

or

Why is this chapter in the Bible?
Why did these events happen?
Why did the people act this way?

Does this verse reveal anything about God/Jesus/Holy Spirit?
Are there examples to follow or avoid? What does this chapter have to teach me?

How can I apply insights from this verse today? This week?

Notes, quotes, doodles, checklists, prayers, etc.

#Iwillmeditate

☐ pray before beginning

Exodus 23　　　　　　　　　Date:

Summarize the main idea(s) in this chapter:

Verse(s) that stood out　　　　or　　　　Who is in this chapter?
　　　　　　　　　　　　　　　　　　　　What do they say? What do they do?

Why did I pick this verse?　　　　or　　　　What is going on?
　　　　　　　　　　　　　　　　　　　　Is there anything going wrong?

Definitions of words and/or　　　　or　　　　When and where
cross references from my verse　　　　　　　　did this happen?

#Iwillmeditate

Rewrite the verse in your own words or personalize it.   or   Why is this chapter in the Bible?
Why did these events happen?
Why did the people act this way?

Does this verse reveal anything about God/Jesus/Holy Spirit?
Are there examples to follow or avoid? What does this chapter have to teach me?

How can I apply insights from this verse today? This week?

Notes, quotes, doodles, checklists, prayers, etc.

#Iwillmeditate

☐ pray before beginning

Exodus 24

Date:

Summarize the main idea(s) in this chapter:

Verse(s) that stood out   or   **Who is in this chapter? What do they say? What do they do?**

Why did I pick this verse?   or   **What is going on? Is there anything going wrong?**

Definitions of words and/or cross references from my verse   or   **When and where did this happen?**

#Iwillmeditate

Rewrite the verse in your own words or personalize it.   or   Why is this chapter in the Bible?
Why did these events happen?
Why did the people act this way?

Does this verse reveal anything about God/Jesus/Holy Spirit?
Are there examples to follow or avoid? What does this chapter have to teach me?

How can I apply insights from this verse today? This week?

Notes, quotes, doodles, checklists, prayers, etc.

#Iwillmeditate

☐ pray before beginning

Exodus 25   Date:

Summarize the main idea(s) in this chapter:

Verse(s) that stood out   or   Who is in this chapter?
What do they say? What do they do?

Why did I pick this verse?   or   What is going on?
Is there anything going wrong?

Definitions of words and/or   or   When and where
cross references from my verse   did this happen?

#Iwillmeditate

Rewrite the verse in your own words   or   Why is this chapter in the Bible?
or personalize it.   Why did these events happen?
                                                                                   Why did the people act this way?

Does this verse reveal anything about God/Jesus/Holy Spirit?
Are there examples to follow or avoid? What does this chapter have to teach me?

How can I apply insights from this verse today? This week?

Notes, quotes, doodles, checklists, prayers, etc.

#Iwillmeditate

☐ pray before beginning

Exodus 26

Date:

Summarize the main idea(s) in this chapter:

Verse(s) that stood out   or   Who is in this chapter? What do they say? What do they do?

Why did I pick this verse?   or   What is going on? Is there anything going wrong?

Definitions of words and/or cross references from my verse   or   When and where did this happen?

#Iwillmeditate

Rewrite the verse in your own words or personalize it.   or   Why is this chapter in the Bible?
Why did these events happen?
Why did the people act this way?

Does this verse reveal anything about God/Jesus/Holy Spirit?
Are there examples to follow or avoid? What does this chapter have to teach me?

How can I apply insights from this verse today? This week?

Notes, quotes, doodles, checklists, prayers, etc.

#Iwillmeditate

☐ pray before beginning

Review and reflect #15

Date:

Review each of the last six days work. Write or list the main takeaway you got from each chapter. (Look closely at the sections "What does this reveal about God?" and "How can I apply this?")

Are there any themes showing up in this week's work?

Are there any areas God is wanting to grow my faith or trust?
Are there any insights from this week's work on how to do this?

Are there any sins God is spotlighting in my life?
Are there any insights from this week's work on how to kill these sins?

#Iwillmeditate

Re-read one or two of the most impactful verses from this week and turn them into a prayer. (There is room on the next pages to write it down if you want.)

How can I thank or praise God as a result of what I've learned this week?

How can I apply what I've learned this week to my life today and next week?

Where do I need His strength for today? Tomorrow? Next week?

Is there a verse from this week that I should commit to memory? Write it on the next page or on a 3x5 card to take with you to memorize.

Are there any sins I need to confess to God in prayer?

Is there anyone I need to forgive? Is there anyone I need to ask forgiveness of?

Are there any seeds of bitterness starting to take root in my heart?

Are there any fears or worries I need to lay at His feet?

notes, verses to memorize

prayers, doodles, etc

☐ pray before beginning

Exodus 27

Date:

Summarize the main idea(s) in this chapter:

Verse(s) that stood out or **Who is in this chapter? What do they say? What do they do?**

Why did I pick this verse? or **What is going on? Is there anything going wrong?**

Definitions of words and/or cross references from my verse or **When and where did this happen?**

#Iwillmeditate

Rewrite the verse in your own words   or   Why is this chapter in the Bible?
or personalize it.   Why did these events happen?
                                             Why did the people act this way?

Does this verse reveal anything about God/Jesus/Holy Spirit?
Are there examples to follow or avoid? What does this chapter have to teach me?

How can I apply insights from this verse today? This week?

Notes, quotes, doodles, checklists, prayers, etc.

#Iwillmeditate

☐ pray before beginning

Exodus 28

Date:

Summarize the main idea(s) in this chapter:

Verse(s) that stood out or **Who is in this chapter? What do they say? What do they do?**

Why did I pick this verse? or **What is going on? Is there anything going wrong?**

Definitions of words and/or cross references from my verse or **When and where did this happen?**

#Iwillmeditate

Rewrite the verse in your own words   or   Why is this chapter in the Bible?
or personalize it.   Why did these events happen?
                                                Why did the people act this way?

Does this verse reveal anything about God/Jesus/Holy Spirit?
Are there examples to follow or avoid? What does this chapter have to teach me?

How can I apply insights from this verse today? This week?

Notes, quotes, doodles, checklists, prayers, etc.

#Iwillmeditate

☐ pray before beginning

Exodus 29

Date:

Summarize the main idea(s) in this chapter:

Verse(s) that stood out or **Who is in this chapter? What do they say? What do they do?**

Why did I pick this verse? or **What is going on? Is there anything going wrong?**

Definitions of words and/or cross references from my verse or **When and where did this happen?**

#Iwillmeditate

Rewrite the verse in your own words or personalize it.   or   Why is this chapter in the Bible?
Why did these events happen?
Why did the people act this way?

Does this verse reveal anything about God/Jesus/Holy Spirit?
Are there examples to follow or avoid? What does this chapter have to teach me?

How can I apply insights from this verse today? This week?

Notes, quotes, doodles, checklists, prayers, etc.

#Iwillmeditate

☐ pray before beginning

Exodus 30

Date:

Summarize the main idea(s) in this chapter:

Verse(s) that stood out **or** Who is in this chapter? What do they say? What do they do?

Why did I pick this verse? **or** What is going on? Is there anything going wrong?

Definitions of words and/or cross references from my verse **or** When and where did this happen?

#Iwillmeditate

Rewrite the verse in your own words or Why is this chapter in the Bible?
or personalize it. Why did these events happen?
 Why did the people act this way?

Does this verse reveal anything about God/Jesus/Holy Spirit?
Are there examples to follow or avoid? What does this chapter have to teach me?

How can I apply insights from this verse today? This week?

Notes, quotes, doodles, checklists, prayers, etc.

#Iwillmeditate

☐ pray before beginning

Exodus 31
Date:

Summarize the main idea(s) in this chapter:

Verse(s) that stood out or **Who is in this chapter? What do they say? What do they do?**

Why did I pick this verse? or **What is going on? Is there anything going wrong?**

Definitions of words and/or cross references from my verse or **When and where did this happen?**

#Iwillmeditate

Rewrite the verse in your own words   or   Why is this chapter in the Bible?
or personalize it.   Why did these events happen?
                                              Why did the people act this way?

Does this verse reveal anything about God/Jesus/Holy Spirit?
Are there examples to follow or avoid? What does this chapter have to teach me?

How can I apply insights from this verse today? This week?

Notes, quotes, doodles, checklists, prayers, etc.

#Iwillmeditate

☐ pray before beginning

Exodus 32

Date:

Summarize the main idea(s) in this chapter:

Verse(s) that stood out or **Who is in this chapter? What do they say? What do they do?**

Why did I pick this verse? or **What is going on? Is there anything going wrong?**

Definitions of words and/or cross references from my verse or **When and where did this happen?**

#Iwillmeditate

Rewrite the verse in your own words   or   Why is this chapter in the Bible?
or personalize it.   Why did these events happen?
                                                                        Why did the people act this way?

Does this verse reveal anything about God/Jesus/Holy Spirit?
Are there examples to follow or avoid? What does this chapter have to teach me?

How can I apply insights from this verse today? This week?

Notes, quotes, doodles, checklists, prayers, etc.

☐ pray before beginning

Review and reflect #16

Date:

Review each of the last six days work. Write or list the main takeaway you got from each chapter. (Look closely at the sections "What does this reveal about God?" and "How can I apply this?")

Are there any themes showing up in this week's work?

Are there any areas God is wanting to grow my faith or trust?
Are there any insights from this week's work on how to do this?

Are there any sins God is spotlighting in my life?
Are there any insights from this week's work on how to kill these sins?

#Iwillmeditate

Re-read one or two of the most impactful verses from this week and turn them into a prayer. (There is room on the next pages to write it down if you want.)

How can I thank or praise God as a result of what I've learned this week?

How can I apply what I've learned this week to my life today and next week?

Where do I need His strength for today? Tomorrow? Next week?

Is there a verse from this week that I should commit to memory? Write it on the next page or on a 3x5 card to take with you to memorize.

Are there any sins I need to confess to God in prayer?

Is there anyone I need to forgive? Is there anyone I need to ask forgiveness of?

Are there any seeds of bitterness starting to take root in my heart?

Are there any fears or worries I need to lay at His feet?

notes, verses to memorize

prayers, doodles, etc

☐ pray before beginning

Exodus 33

Date:

Summarize the main idea(s) in this chapter:

Verse(s) that stood out   or   Who is in this chapter? What do they say? What do they do?

Why did I pick this verse?   or   What is going on? Is there anything going wrong?

Definitions of words and/or cross references from my verse   or   When and where did this happen?

#Iwillmeditate

Rewrite the verse in your own words   or   Why is this chapter in the Bible?
or personalize it.   Why did these events happen?
                                            Why did the people act this way?

Does this verse reveal anything about God/Jesus/Holy Spirit?
Are there examples to follow or avoid? What does this chapter have to teach me?

How can I apply insights from this verse today? This week?

Notes, quotes, doodles, checklists, prayers, etc.

#Iwillmeditate

☐ pray before beginning

Exodus 34

Date:

Summarize the main idea(s) in this chapter:

Verse(s) that stood out   or   Who is in this chapter?
What do they say? What do they do?

Why did I pick this verse?   or   What is going on?
Is there anything going wrong?

Definitions of words and/or   or   When and where
cross references from my verse   did this happen?

#Iwillmeditate

Rewrite the verse in your own words　　or　　Why is this chapter in the Bible?
or personalize it.　　　　　　　　　　　　　Why did these events happen?
　　　　　　　　　　　　　　　　　　　　　　Why did the people act this way?

Does this verse reveal anything about God/Jesus/Holy Spirit?
Are there examples to follow or avoid? What does this chapter have to teach me?

How can I apply insights from this verse today? This week?

Notes, quotes, doodles, checklists, prayers, etc.

#Iwillmeditate

☐ pray before beginning

Exodus 35 Date:

Summarize the main idea(s) in this chapter:

Verse(s) that stood out　　or　　Who is in this chapter?
What do they say? What do they do?

Why did I pick this verse?　　or　　What is going on?
Is there anything going wrong?

Definitions of words and/or　　or　　When and where
cross references from my verse　　　did this happen?

#Iwillmeditate

Rewrite the verse in your own words　　or　　Why is this chapter in the Bible?
or personalize it.　　　　　　　　　　　　Why did these events happen?
　　　　　　　　　　　　　　　　　　　　Why did the people act this way?

Does this verse reveal anything about God/Jesus/Holy Spirit?
Are there examples to follow or avoid? What does this chapter have to teach me?

How can I apply insights from this verse today? This week?

Notes, quotes, doodles, checklists, prayers, etc.

#Iwillmeditate

☐ pray before beginning

Exodus 36

Date:

Summarize the main idea(s) in this chapter:

Verse(s) that stood out or **Who is in this chapter? What do they say? What do they do?**

Why did I pick this verse? or **What is going on? Is there anything going wrong?**

Definitions of words and/or cross references from my verse or **When and where did this happen?**

#Iwillmeditate

Rewrite the verse in your own words or Why is this chapter in the Bible?
or personalize it. Why did these events happen?
  Why did the people act this way?

Does this verse reveal anything about God/Jesus/Holy Spirit?
Are there examples to follow or avoid? What does this chapter have to teach me?

How can I apply insights from this verse today? This week?

Notes, quotes, doodles, checklists, prayers, etc.

#Iwillmeditate

☐ pray before beginning

Exodus 37

Date:

Summarize the main idea(s) in this chapter:

Verse(s) that stood out or **Who is in this chapter? What do they say? What do they do?**

Why did I pick this verse? or **What is going on? Is there anything going wrong?**

Definitions of words and/or cross references from my verse or **When and where did this happen?**

#Iwillmeditate

Rewrite the verse in your own words   or   Why is this chapter in the Bible?
or personalize it.   Why did these events happen?
                                                      Why did the people act this way?

Does this verse reveal anything about God/Jesus/Holy Spirit?
Are there examples to follow or avoid? What does this chapter have to teach me?

How can I apply insights from this verse today? This week?

Notes, quotes, doodles, checklists, prayers, etc.

#Iwillmeditate

☐ pray before beginning

Exodus 38

Date:

Summarize the main idea(s) in this chapter:

Verse(s) that stood out or **Who is in this chapter? What do they say? What do they do?**

Why did I pick this verse? or **What is going on? Is there anything going wrong?**

Definitions of words and/or cross references from my verse or **When and where did this happen?**

#Iwillmeditate

Rewrite the verse in your own words or personalize it.

or

Why is this chapter in the Bible?
Why did these events happen?
Why did the people act this way?

Does this verse reveal anything about God/Jesus/Holy Spirit?
Are there examples to follow or avoid? What does this chapter have to teach me?

How can I apply insights from this verse today? This week?

Notes, quotes, doodles, checklists, prayers, etc.

#Iwillmeditate

☐ pray before beginning

Review and reflect #17

Date:

Review each of the last six days work. Write or list the main takeaway you got from each chapter. (Look closely at the sections "What does this reveal about God?" and "How can I apply this?")

Are there any themes showing up in this week's work?

Are there any areas God is wanting to grow my faith or trust?
Are there any insights from this week's work on how to do this?

Are there any sins God is spotlighting in my life?
Are there any insights from this week's work on how to kill these sins?

#Iwillmeditate

Re-read one or two of the most impactful verses from this week and turn them into a prayer. (There is room on the next pages to write it down if you want.)

How can I thank or praise God as a result of what I've learned this week?

How can I apply what I've learned this week to my life today and next week?

Where do I need His strength for today? Tomorrow? Next week?

Is there a verse from this week that I should commit to memory? Write it on the next page or on a 3x5 card to take with you to memorize.

Are there any sins I need to confess to God in prayer?

Is there anyone I need to forgive? Is there anyone I need to ask forgiveness of?

Are there any seeds of bitterness starting to take root in my heart?

Are there any fears or worries I need to lay at His feet?

notes, verses to memorize

prayers, doodles, etc

☐ pray before beginning

Exodus 39

Date:

Summarize the main idea(s) in this chapter:

Verse(s) that stood out   or   **Who is in this chapter? What do they say? What do they do?**

Why did I pick this verse?   or   **What is going on? Is there anything going wrong?**

Definitions of words and/or cross references from my verse   or   **When and where did this happen?**

#Iwillmeditate

Rewrite the verse in your own words or personalize it.   or   Why is this chapter in the Bible? Why did these events happen? Why did the people act this way?

Does this verse reveal anything about God/Jesus/Holy Spirit? Are there examples to follow or avoid? What does this chapter have to teach me?

How can I apply insights from this verse today? This week?

Notes, quotes, doodles, checklists, prayers, etc.

#Iwillmeditate

☐ pray before beginning

Exodus 40

Date:

Summarize the main idea(s) in this chapter:

Verse(s) that stood out or **Who is in this chapter? What do they say? What do they do?**

Why did I pick this verse? or **What is going on? Is there anything going wrong?**

Definitions of words and/or cross references from my verse or **When and where did this happen?**

#Iwillmeditate

Rewrite the verse in your own words   or   Why is this chapter in the Bible?
or personalize it.   Why did these events happen?
                                            Why did the people act this way?

Does this verse reveal anything about God/Jesus/Holy Spirit?
Are there examples to follow or avoid? What does this chapter have to teach me?

How can I apply insights from this verse today? This week?

Notes, quotes, doodles, checklists, prayers, etc.

#Iwillmeditate

☐ pray before beginning

Mark 1

Date:

Summarize the main idea(s) in this chapter:

Verse(s) that stood out   or   Who is in this chapter? What do they say? What do they do?

Why did I pick this verse?   or   What is going on? Is there anything going wrong?

Definitions of words and/or cross references from my verse   or   When and where did this happen?

#Iwillmeditate

Rewrite the verse in your own words   or   Why is this chapter in the Bible?
or personalize it.   Why did these events happen?
                                                                    Why did the people act this way?

Does this verse reveal anything about God/Jesus/Holy Spirit?
Are there examples to follow or avoid? What does this chapter have to teach me?

How can I apply insights from this verse today? This week?

Notes, quotes, doodles, checklists, prayers, etc.

#Iwillmeditate

☐ pray before beginning

Mark 2

Date:

Summarize the main idea(s) in this chapter:

Verse(s) that stood out or **Who is in this chapter? What do they say? What do they do?**

Why did I pick this verse? or **What is going on? Is there anything going wrong?**

Definitions of words and/or cross references from my verse or **When and where did this happen?**

#Iwillmeditate

Rewrite the verse in your own words or personalize it.   or   Why is this chapter in the Bible? Why did these events happen? Why did the people act this way?

Does this verse reveal anything about God/Jesus/Holy Spirit?
Are there examples to follow or avoid? What does this chapter have to teach me?

How can I apply insights from this verse today? This week?

Notes, quotes, doodles, checklists, prayers, etc.

#Iwillmeditate

☐ pray before beginning

Mark 3

Date:

Summarize the main idea(s) in this chapter:

Verse(s) that stood out or **Who is in this chapter? What do they say? What do they do?**

Why did I pick this verse? or **What is going on? Is there anything going wrong?**

Definitions of words and/or cross references from my verse or **When and where did this happen?**

#Iwillmeditate

Rewrite the verse in your own words or personalize it. or Why is this chapter in the Bible? Why did these events happen? Why did the people act this way?

Does this verse reveal anything about God/Jesus/Holy Spirit?
Are there examples to follow or avoid? What does this chapter have to teach me?

How can I apply insights from this verse today? This week?

Notes, quotes, doodles, checklists, prayers, etc.

#Iwillmeditate

☐ pray before beginning

Mark 4

Date:

Summarize the main idea(s) in this chapter:

Verse(s) that stood out   or   **Who is in this chapter? What do they say? What do they do?**

Why did I pick this verse?   or   **What is going on? Is there anything going wrong?**

Definitions of words and/or cross references from my verse   or   **When and where did this happen?**

#Iwillmeditate

Rewrite the verse in your own words   or   Why is this chapter in the Bible?
or personalize it.   Why did these events happen?
                                                                     Why did the people act this way?

Does this verse reveal anything about God/Jesus/Holy Spirit?
Are there examples to follow or avoid? What does this chapter have to teach me?

How can I apply insights from this verse today? This week?

Notes, quotes, doodles, checklists, prayers, etc.

#Iwillmeditate

☐ pray before beginning

Review and reflect #18

Date:

Review each of the last six days work. Write or list the main takeaway you got from each chapter. (Look closely at the sections "What does this reveal about God?" and "How can I apply this?")

Are there any themes showing up in this week's work?

Are there any areas God is wanting to grow my faith or trust?
Are there any insights from this week's work on how to do this?

Are there any sins God is spotlighting in my life?
Are there any insights from this week's work on how to kill these sins?

#Iwillmeditate

Re-read one or two of the most impactful verses from this week and turn them into a prayer. (There is room on the next pages to write it down if you want.)

How can I thank or praise God as a result of what I've learned this week?

How can I apply what I've learned this week to my life today and next week?

Where do I need His strength for today? Tomorrow? Next week?

Is there a verse from this week that I should commit to memory? Write it on the next page or on a 3x5 card to take with you to memorize.

Are there any sins I need to confess to God in prayer?

Is there anyone I need to forgive? Is there anyone I need to ask forgiveness of?

Are there any seeds of bitterness starting to take root in my heart?

Are there any fears or worries I need to lay at His feet?

notes, verses to memorize

prayers, doodles, etc

☐ pray before beginning

Mark 5

Date:

Summarize the main idea(s) in this chapter:

Verse(s) that stood out   or   **Who is in this chapter? What do they say? What do they do?**

Why did I pick this verse?   or   **What is going on? Is there anything going wrong?**

Definitions of words and/or cross references from my verse   or   **When and where did this happen?**

#Iwillmeditate

Rewrite the verse in your own words or personalize it.   **or**   Why is this chapter in the Bible?
Why did these events happen?
Why did the people act this way?

Does this verse reveal anything about God/Jesus/Holy Spirit?
Are there examples to follow or avoid? What does this chapter have to teach me?

How can I apply insights from this verse today? This week?

Notes, quotes, doodles, checklists, prayers, etc.

#Iwillmeditate

☐ pray before beginning

Mark 6

Date:

Summarize the main idea(s) in this chapter:

Verse(s) that stood out or Who is in this chapter?
What do they say? What do they do?

Why did I pick this verse? or What is going on?
Is there anything going wrong?

Definitions of words and/or or When and where
cross references from my verse did this happen?

#Iwillmeditate

Rewrite the verse in your own words or personalize it.

or

Why is this chapter in the Bible?
Why did these events happen?
Why did the people act this way?

Does this verse reveal anything about God/Jesus/Holy Spirit?
Are there examples to follow or avoid? What does this chapter have to teach me?

How can I apply insights from this verse today? This week?

Notes, quotes, doodles, checklists, prayers, etc.

#Iwillmeditate

☐ pray before beginning

Mark 7

Date:

Summarize the main idea(s) in this chapter:

Verse(s) that stood out or **Who is in this chapter? What do they say? What do they do?**

Why did I pick this verse? or **What is going on? Is there anything going wrong?**

Definitions of words and/or cross references from my verse or **When and where did this happen?**

#Iwillmeditate

Rewrite the verse in your own words   or   Why is this chapter in the Bible?
or personalize it.   Why did these events happen?
                                                                   Why did the people act this way?

Does this verse reveal anything about God/Jesus/Holy Spirit?
Are there examples to follow or avoid? What does this chapter have to teach me?

How can I apply insights from this verse today? This week?

Notes, quotes, doodles, checklists, prayers, etc.

#Iwillmeditate

☐ pray before beginning

Date:

Summarize the main idea(s) in this chapter:

Verse(s) that stood out   or   Who is in this chapter?
What do they say? What do they do?

Why did I pick this verse?   or   What is going on?
Is there anything going wrong?

Definitions of words and/or   or   When and where
cross references from my verse   did this happen?

#Iwillmeditate

Rewrite the verse in your own words or personalize it.   or   Why is this chapter in the Bible?
Why did these events happen?
Why did the people act this way?

Does this verse reveal anything about God/Jesus/Holy Spirit?
Are there examples to follow or avoid? What does this chapter have to teach me?

How can I apply insights from this verse today? This week?

Notes, quotes, doodles, checklists, prayers, etc.

☐ pray before beginning

Mark 9

Date:

Summarize the main idea(s) in this chapter:

Verse(s) that stood out   or   **Who is in this chapter? What do they say? What do they do?**

Why did I pick this verse?   or   **What is going on? Is there anything going wrong?**

Definitions of words and/or cross references from my verse   or   **When and where did this happen?**

#Iwillmeditate

Rewrite the verse in your own words　　or　　Why is this chapter in the Bible?
or personalize it.　　　　　　　　　　　　　Why did these events happen?
　　　　　　　　　　　　　　　　　　　　　　Why did the people act this way?

Does this verse reveal anything about God/Jesus/Holy Spirit?
Are there examples to follow or avoid? What does this chapter have to teach me?

How can I apply insights from this verse today? This week?

Notes, quotes, doodles, checklists, prayers, etc.

#Iwillmeditate

☐ pray before beginning

Mark 10

Date:

Summarize the main idea(s) in this chapter:

Verse(s) that stood out   or   **Who is in this chapter? What do they say? What do they do?**

Why did I pick this verse?   or   **What is going on? Is there anything going wrong?**

Definitions of words and/or cross references from my verse   or   **When and where did this happen?**

#Iwillmeditate

Rewrite the verse in your own words or Why is this chapter in the Bible?
or personalize it.   Why did these events happen?
                                          Why did the people act this way?

Does this verse reveal anything about God/Jesus/Holy Spirit?
Are there examples to follow or avoid? What does this chapter have to teach me?

How can I apply insights from this verse today? This week?

Notes, quotes, doodles, checklists, prayers, etc.

#Iwillmeditate

☐ pray before beginning

Review and reflect #19

Date:

Review each of the last six days work. Write or list the main takeaway you got from each chapter. (Look closely at the sections "What does this reveal about God?" and "How can I apply this?")

Are there any themes showing up in this week's work?

Are there any areas God is wanting to grow my faith or trust?
Are there any insights from this week's work on how to do this?

Are there any sins God is spotlighting in my life?
Are there any insights from this week's work on how to kill these sins?

#Iwillmeditate

Re-read one or two of the most impactful verses from this week and turn them into a prayer. (There is room on the next pages to write it down if you want.)

How can I thank or praise God as a result of what I've learned this week?

How can I apply what I've learned this week to my life today and next week?

Where do I need His strength for today? Tomorrow? Next week?

Is there a verse from this week that I should commit to memory? Write it on the next page or on a 3x5 card to take with you to memorize.

Are there any sins I need to confess to God in prayer?

Is there anyone I need to forgive? Is there anyone I need to ask forgiveness of?

Are there any seeds of bitterness starting to take root in my heart?

Are there any fears or worries I need to lay at His feet?

notes, verses to memorize

prayers, doodles, etc

☐ pray before beginning

Mark 11

Date:

Summarize the main idea(s) in this chapter:

Verse(s) that stood out   or   **Who is in this chapter? What do they say? What do they do?**

Why did I pick this verse?   or   **What is going on? Is there anything going wrong?**

Definitions of words and/or cross references from my verse   or   **When and where did this happen?**

#Iwillmeditate

Rewrite the verse in your own words　　or　　Why is this chapter in the Bible?
or personalize it.　　　　　　　　　　　　　Why did these events happen?
　　　　　　　　　　　　　　　　　　　　　Why did the people act this way?

Does this verse reveal anything about God/Jesus/Holy Spirit?
Are there examples to follow or avoid? What does this chapter have to teach me?

How can I apply insights from this verse today? This week?

Notes, quotes, doodles, checklists, prayers, etc.

☐ pray before beginning

Mark 12

Date:

Summarize the main idea(s) in this chapter:

| Verse(s) that stood out | or | Who is in this chapter? What do they say? What do they do? |

| Why did I pick this verse? | or | What is going on? Is there anything going wrong? |

| Definitions of words and/or cross references from my verse | or | When and where did this happen? |

#Iwillmeditate

Rewrite the verse in your own words or personalize it.   or   Why is this chapter in the Bible? Why did these events happen? Why did the people act this way?

Does this verse reveal anything about God/Jesus/Holy Spirit?
Are there examples to follow or avoid? What does this chapter have to teach me?

How can I apply insights from this verse today? This week?

Notes, quotes, doodles, checklists, prayers, etc.

☐ pray before beginning

Mark 13

Date:

Summarize the main idea(s) in this chapter:

Verse(s) that stood out or **Who is in this chapter? What do they say? What do they do?**

Why did I pick this verse? or **What is going on? Is there anything going wrong?**

Definitions of words and/or cross references from my verse or **When and where did this happen?**

#Iwillmeditate

Rewrite the verse in your own words or Why is this chapter in the Bible?
or personalize it. Why did these events happen?
Why did the people act this way?

Does this verse reveal anything about God/Jesus/Holy Spirit?
Are there examples to follow or avoid? What does this chapter have to teach me?

How can I apply insights from this verse today? This week?

Notes, quotes, doodles, checklists, prayers, etc.

#Iwillmeditate

☐ pray before beginning

Mark 14

Date:

Summarize the main idea(s) in this chapter:

Verse(s) that stood out   or   **Who is in this chapter? What do they say? What do they do?**

Why did I pick this verse?   or   **What is going on? Is there anything going wrong?**

Definitions of words and/or cross references from my verse   or   **When and where did this happen?**

#Iwillmeditate

Rewrite the verse in your own words   or   Why is this chapter in the Bible?
or personalize it.   Why did these events happen?
   Why did the people act this way?

Does this verse reveal anything about God/Jesus/Holy Spirit?
Are there examples to follow or avoid? What does this chapter have to teach me?

How can I apply insights from this verse today? This week?

Notes, quotes, doodles, checklists, prayers, etc.

#Iwillmeditate

☐ pray before beginning

Mark 15

Date:

Summarize the main idea(s) in this chapter:

Verse(s) that stood out or Who is in this chapter? What do they say? What do they do?

Why did I pick this verse? or What is going on? Is there anything going wrong?

Definitions of words and/or cross references from my verse or When and where did this happen?

#Iwillmeditate

Rewrite the verse in your own words　　or　　Why is this chapter in the Bible?
or personalize it.　　　　　　　　　　　　　Why did these events happen?
　　　　　　　　　　　　　　　　　　　　　Why did the people act this way?

Does this verse reveal anything about God/Jesus/Holy Spirit?
Are there examples to follow or avoid? What does this chapter have to teach me?

How can I apply insights from this verse today? This week?

Notes, quotes, doodles, checklists, prayers, etc.

#Iwillmeditate

☐ pray before beginning

Mark 16

Date:

Summarize the main idea(s) in this chapter:

Verse(s) that stood out or **Who is in this chapter? What do they say? What do they do?**

Why did I pick this verse? or **What is going on? Is there anything going wrong?**

Definitions of words and/or cross references from my verse or **When and where did this happen?**

#Iwillmeditate

Rewrite the verse in your own words or Why is this chapter in the Bible?
or personalize it. Why did these events happen?
 Why did the people act this way?

Does this verse reveal anything about God/Jesus/Holy Spirit?
Are there examples to follow or avoid? What does this chapter have to teach me?

How can I apply insights from this verse today? This week?

Notes, quotes, doodles, checklists, prayers, etc.

#Iwillmeditate

☐ pray before beginning

Review and reflect #20

Date:

Review each of the last six days work. Write or list the main takeaway you got from each chapter. (Look closely at the sections "What does this reveal about God?" and "How can I apply this?")

Are there any themes showing up in this week's work?

Are there any areas God is wanting to grow my faith or trust?
Are there any insights from this week's work on how to do this?

Are there any sins God is spotlighting in my life?
Are there any insights from this week's work on how to kill these sins?

#Iwillmeditate

Re-read one or two of the most impactful verses from this week and turn them into a prayer. (There is room on the next pages to write it down if you want.)

How can I thank or praise God as a result of what I've learned this week?

How can I apply what I've learned this week to my life today and next week?

Where do I need His strength for today? Tomorrow? Next week?

Is there a verse from this week that I should commit to memory? Write it on the next page or on a 3x5 card to take with you to memorize.

Are there any sins I need to confess to God in prayer?

Is there anyone I need to forgive? Is there anyone I need to ask forgiveness of?

Are there any seeds of bitterness starting to take root in my heart?

Are there any fears or worries I need to lay at His feet?

notes, verses to memorize

prayers, doodles, etc

☐ pray before beginning

Leviticus 1-2

Date:

Summarize the main idea(s) in this chapter:

Verse(s) that stood out or **Who is in this chapter? What do they say? What do they do?**

Why did I pick this verse? or **What is going on? Is there anything going wrong?**

Definitions of words and/or cross references from my verse or **When and where did this happen?**

#Iwillmeditate

Rewrite the verse in your own words or Why is this chapter in the Bible?
or personalize it. Why did these events happen?
Why did the people act this way?

Does this verse reveal anything about God/Jesus/Holy Spirit?
Are there examples to follow or avoid? What does this chapter have to teach me?

How can I apply insights from this verse today? This week?

Notes, quotes, doodles, checklists, prayers, etc.

#Iwillmeditate

☐ pray before beginning

Leviticus 3

Date:

Summarize the main idea(s) in this chapter:

Verse(s) that stood out or **Who is in this chapter? What do they say? What do they do?**

Why did I pick this verse? or **What is going on? Is there anything going wrong?**

Definitions of words and/or cross references from my verse or **When and where did this happen?**

#Iwillmeditate

Rewrite the verse in your own words   or   Why is this chapter in the Bible?
or personalize it.   Why did these events happen?
                                            Why did the people act this way?

Does this verse reveal anything about God/Jesus/Holy Spirit?
Are there examples to follow or avoid? What does this chapter have to teach me?

How can I apply insights from this verse today? This week?

Notes, quotes, doodles, checklists, prayers, etc.

#Iwillmeditate

☐ pray before beginning

Leviticus 4

Date:

Summarize the main idea(s) in this chapter:

Verse(s) that stood out or **Who is in this chapter? What do they say? What do they do?**

Why did I pick this verse? or **What is going on? Is there anything going wrong?**

Definitions of words and/or cross references from my verse or **When and where did this happen?**

#Iwillmeditate

Rewrite the verse in your own words or Why is this chapter in the Bible?
or personalize it. Why did these events happen?
Why did the people act this way?

Does this verse reveal anything about God/Jesus/Holy Spirit?
Are there examples to follow or avoid? What does this chapter have to teach me?

How can I apply insights from this verse today? This week?

Notes, quotes, doodles, checklists, prayers, etc.

#Iwillmeditate

☐ pray before beginning

Leviticus 5

Date:

Summarize the main idea(s) in this chapter:

Verse(s) that stood out   or   **Who is in this chapter? What do they say? What do they do?**

Why did I pick this verse?   or   **What is going on? Is there anything going wrong?**

Definitions of words and/or cross references from my verse   or   **When and where did this happen?**

#Iwillmeditate

Rewrite the verse in your own words   or   Why is this chapter in the Bible?
or personalize it.   Why did these events happen?
   Why did the people act this way?

Does this verse reveal anything about God/Jesus/Holy Spirit?
Are there examples to follow or avoid? What does this chapter have to teach me?

How can I apply insights from this verse today? This week?

Notes, quotes, doodles, checklists, prayers, etc.

☐ pray before beginning

Leviticus 6

Date:

Summarize the main idea(s) in this chapter:

Verse(s) that stood out   or   **Who is in this chapter? What do they say? What do they do?**

Why did I pick this verse?   or   **What is going on? Is there anything going wrong?**

Definitions of words and/or cross references from my verse   or   **When and where did this happen?**

#Iwillmeditate

Rewrite the verse in your own words or Why is this chapter in the Bible?
or personalize it. Why did these events happen?
  Why did the people act this way?

Does this verse reveal anything about God/Jesus/Holy Spirit?
Are there examples to follow or avoid? What does this chapter have to teach me?

How can I apply insights from this verse today? This week?

Notes, quotes, doodles, checklists, prayers, etc.

#Iwillmeditate

☐ pray before beginning

Leviticus 7

Date:

Summarize the main idea(s) in this chapter:

Verse(s) that stood out or **Who is in this chapter? What do they say? What do they do?**

Why did I pick this verse? or **What is going on? Is there anything going wrong?**

Definitions of words and/or cross references from my verse or **When and where did this happen?**

#Iwillmeditate

Rewrite the verse in your own words or personalize it.   or   Why is this chapter in the Bible?
Why did these events happen?
Why did the people act this way?

Does this verse reveal anything about God/Jesus/Holy Spirit?
Are there examples to follow or avoid? What does this chapter have to teach me?

How can I apply insights from this verse today? This week?

Notes, quotes, doodles, checklists, prayers, etc.

#Iwillmeditate

☐ pray before beginning

Review and reflect #21

Date:

Review each of the last six days work. Write or list the main takeaway you got from each chapter. (Look closely at the sections "What does this reveal about God?" and "How can I apply this?")

Are there any themes showing up in this week's work?

Are there any areas God is wanting to grow my faith or trust?
Are there any insights from this week's work on how to do this?

Are there any sins God is spotlighting in my life?
Are there any insights from this week's work on how to kill these sins?

Re-read one or two of the most impactful verses from this week and turn them into a prayer. (There is room on the next pages to write it down if you want.)

How can I thank or praise God as a result of what I've learned this week?

How can I apply what I've learned this week to my life today and next week?

Where do I need His strength for today? Tomorrow? Next week?

Is there a verse from this week that I should commit to memory? Write it on the next page or on a 3x5 card to take with you to memorize.

Are there any sins I need to confess to God in prayer?

Is there anyone I need to forgive? Is there anyone I need to ask forgiveness of?

Are there any seeds of bitterness starting to take root in my heart?

Are there any fears or worries I need to lay at His feet?

notes, verses to memorize

prayers, doodles, etc

☐ pray before beginning

Leviticus 8

Date:

Summarize the main idea(s) in this chapter:

Verse(s) that stood out or **Who is in this chapter? What do they say? What do they do?**

Why did I pick this verse? or **What is going on? Is there anything going wrong?**

Definitions of words and/or cross references from my verse or **When and where did this happen?**

#Iwillmeditate

Rewrite the verse in your own words   or   Why is this chapter in the Bible?
or personalize it.   Why did these events happen?
                                             Why did the people act this way?

Does this verse reveal anything about God/Jesus/Holy Spirit?
Are there examples to follow or avoid? What does this chapter have to teach me?

How can I apply insights from this verse today? This week?

Notes, quotes, doodles, checklists, prayers, etc.

#Iwillmeditate

☐ pray before beginning

Leviticus 9-10

Date:

Summarize the main idea(s) in this chapter:

Verse(s) that stood out   or   Who is in this chapter? What do they say? What do they do?

Why did I pick this verse?   or   What is going on? Is there anything going wrong?

Definitions of words and/or cross references from my verse   or   When and where did this happen?

#Iwillmeditate

Rewrite the verse in your own words or personalize it.   or   Why is this chapter in the Bible?
Why did these events happen?
Why did the people act this way?

Does this verse reveal anything about God/Jesus/Holy Spirit?
Are there examples to follow or avoid? What does this chapter have to teach me?

How can I apply insights from this verse today? This week?

Notes, quotes, doodles, checklists, prayers, etc.

#Iwillmeditate

☐ pray before beginning

Leviticus 11

Date:

Summarize the main idea(s) in this chapter:

Verse(s) that stood out   or   **Who is in this chapter? What do they say? What do they do?**

Why did I pick this verse?   or   **What is going on? Is there anything going wrong?**

Definitions of words and/or cross references from my verse   or   **When and where did this happen?**

#Iwillmeditate

Rewrite the verse in your own words or personalize it.   or   Why is this chapter in the Bible?
Why did these events happen?
Why did the people act this way?

Does this verse reveal anything about God/Jesus/Holy Spirit?
Are there examples to follow or avoid? What does this chapter have to teach me?

How can I apply insights from this verse today? This week?

Notes, quotes, doodles, checklists, prayers, etc.

#Iwillmeditate

☐ pray before beginning

Leviticus 12

Date:

Summarize the main idea(s) in this chapter:

Verse(s) that stood out   or   **Who is in this chapter? What do they say? What do they do?**

Why did I pick this verse?   or   **What is going on? Is there anything going wrong?**

Definitions of words and/or cross references from my verse   or   **When and where did this happen?**

#Iwillmeditate

Rewrite the verse in your own words or personalize it.   or   Why is this chapter in the Bible? Why did these events happen? Why did the people act this way?

Does this verse reveal anything about God/Jesus/Holy Spirit?
Are there examples to follow or avoid? What does this chapter have to teach me?

How can I apply insights from this verse today? This week?

Notes, quotes, doodles, checklists, prayers, etc.

#Iwillmeditate

☐ pray before beginning

Leviticus 13

Date:

Summarize the main idea(s) in this chapter:

Verse(s) that stood out or **Who is in this chapter? What do they say? What do they do?**

Why did I pick this verse? or **What is going on? Is there anything going wrong?**

Definitions of words and/or cross references from my verse or **When and where did this happen?**

#Iwillmeditate

Rewrite the verse in your own words or personalize it.   or   Why is this chapter in the Bible?
Why did these events happen?
Why did the people act this way?

Does this verse reveal anything about God/Jesus/Holy Spirit?
Are there examples to follow or avoid? What does this chapter have to teach me?

How can I apply insights from this verse today? This week?

Notes, quotes, doodles, checklists, prayers, etc.

#Iwillmeditate

☐ pray before beginning

Leviticus 14

Date:

Summarize the main idea(s) in this chapter:

Verse(s) that stood out   or   **Who is in this chapter? What do they say? What do they do?**

Why did I pick this verse?   or   **What is going on? Is there anything going wrong?**

Definitions of words and/or cross references from my verse   or   **When and where did this happen?**

#Iwillmeditate

Rewrite the verse in your own words   or   Why is this chapter in the Bible?
or personalize it.   Why did these events happen?
                                                                              Why did the people act this way?

Does this verse reveal anything about God/Jesus/Holy Spirit?
Are there examples to follow or avoid? What does this chapter have to teach me?

How can I apply insights from this verse today? This week?

Notes, quotes, doodles, checklists, prayers, etc.

#Iwillmeditate

☐ pray before beginning

Review and reflect #22

Date:

Review each of the last six days work. Write or list the main takeaway you got from each chapter. (Look closely at the sections "What does this reveal about God?" and "How can I apply this?")

Are there any themes showing up in this week's work?

Are there any areas God is wanting to grow my faith or trust?
Are there any insights from this week's work on how to do this?

Are there any sins God is spotlighting in my life?
Are there any insights from this week's work on how to kill these sins?

#Iwillmeditate

Re-read one or two of the most impactful verses from this week and turn them into a prayer. (There is room on the next pages to write it down if you want.)

How can I thank or praise God as a result of what I've learned this week?

How can I apply what I've learned this week to my life today and next week?

Where do I need His strength for today? Tomorrow? Next week?

Is there a verse from this week that I should commit to memory? Write it on the next page or on a 3x5 card to take with you to memorize.

Are there any sins I need to confess to God in prayer?

Is there anyone I need to forgive? Is there anyone I need to ask forgiveness of?

Are there any seeds of bitterness starting to take root in my heart?

Are there any fears or worries I need to lay at His feet?

notes, verses to memorize

prayers, doodles, etc

☐ pray before beginning

Leviticus 15

Date:

Summarize the main idea(s) in this chapter:

Verse(s) that stood out or Who is in this chapter?
 What do they say? What do they do?

Why did I pick this verse? or What is going on?
 Is there anything going wrong?

Definitions of words and/or or When and where
cross references from my verse did this happen?

#Iwillmeditate

Rewrite the verse in your own words   or   Why is this chapter in the Bible?
or personalize it.   Why did these events happen?
                                                         Why did the people act this way?

Does this verse reveal anything about God/Jesus/Holy Spirit?
Are there examples to follow or avoid? What does this chapter have to teach me?

How can I apply insights from this verse today? This week?

Notes, quotes, doodles, checklists, prayers, etc.

#Iwillmeditate

☐ pray before beginning

Leviticus 16

Date:

Summarize the main idea(s) in this chapter:

Verse(s) that stood out or **Who is in this chapter? What do they say? What do they do?**

Why did I pick this verse? or **What is going on? Is there anything going wrong?**

Definitions of words and/or cross references from my verse or **When and where did this happen?**

#Iwillmeditate

Rewrite the verse in your own words or personalize it.   or   Why is this chapter in the Bible?
Why did these events happen?
Why did the people act this way?

Does this verse reveal anything about God/Jesus/Holy Spirit?
Are there examples to follow or avoid? What does this chapter have to teach me?

How can I apply insights from this verse today? This week?

Notes, quotes, doodles, checklists, prayers, etc.

☐ pray before beginning

Leviticus 17

Date:

Summarize the main idea(s) in this chapter:

Verse(s) that stood out   or   Who is in this chapter? What do they say? What do they do?

Why did I pick this verse?   or   What is going on? Is there anything going wrong?

Definitions of words and/or cross references from my verse   or   When and where did this happen?

#Iwillmeditate

Rewrite the verse in your own words or personalize it.   or   Why is this chapter in the Bible?
Why did these events happen?
Why did the people act this way?

Does this verse reveal anything about God/Jesus/Holy Spirit?
Are there examples to follow or avoid? What does this chapter have to teach me?

How can I apply insights from this verse today? This week?

Notes, quotes, doodles, checklists, prayers, etc.

#Iwillmeditate

☐ pray before beginning

Leviticus 18

Date:

Summarize the main idea(s) in this chapter:

Verse(s) that stood out   or   **Who is in this chapter? What do they say? What do they do?**

Why did I pick this verse?   or   **What is going on? Is there anything going wrong?**

Definitions of words and/or cross references from my verse   or   **When and where did this happen?**

#Iwillmeditate

Rewrite the verse in your own words or Why is this chapter in the Bible?
or personalize it. Why did these events happen?
Why did the people act this way?

Does this verse reveal anything about God/Jesus/Holy Spirit?
Are there examples to follow or avoid? What does this chapter have to teach me?

How can I apply insights from this verse today? This week?

Notes, quotes, doodles, checklists, prayers, etc.

#Iwillmeditate

☐ pray before beginning

Leviticus 19

Date:

Summarize the main idea(s) in this chapter:

Verse(s) that stood out   or   **Who is in this chapter? What do they say? What do they do?**

Why did I pick this verse?   or   **What is going on? Is there anything going wrong?**

Definitions of words and/or cross references from my verse   or   **When and where did this happen?**

#Iwillmeditate

Rewrite the verse in your own words   or   Why is this chapter in the Bible?
or personalize it.   Why did these events happen?
                                            Why did the people act this way?

Does this verse reveal anything about God/Jesus/Holy Spirit?
Are there examples to follow or avoid? What does this chapter have to teach me?

How can I apply insights from this verse today? This week?

Notes, quotes, doodles, checklists, prayers, etc.

☐ pray before beginning

Leviticus 20-21

Date:

Summarize the main idea(s) in this chapter:

Verse(s) that stood out or Who is in this chapter? What do they say? What do they do?

Why did I pick this verse? or What is going on? Is there anything going wrong?

Definitions of words and/or cross references from my verse or When and where did this happen?

#Iwillmeditate

Rewrite the verse in your own words or Why is this chapter in the Bible?
or personalize it. Why did these events happen?
Why did the people act this way?

Does this verse reveal anything about God/Jesus/Holy Spirit?
Are there examples to follow or avoid? What does this chapter have to teach me?

How can I apply insights from this verse today? This week?

Notes, quotes, doodles, checklists, prayers, etc.

#Iwillmeditate

☐ pray before beginning

Review and reflect #23

Date:

Review each of the last six days work. Write or list the main takeaway you got from each chapter. (Look closely at the sections "What does this reveal about God?" and "How can I apply this?")

Are there any themes showing up in this week's work?

Are there any areas God is wanting to grow my faith or trust?
Are there any insights from this week's work on how to do this?

Are there any sins God is spotlighting in my life?
Are there any insights from this week's work on how to kill these sins?

#Iwillmeditate

Re-read one or two of the most impactful verses from this week and turn them into a prayer. (There is room on the next pages to write it down if you want.)

How can I thank or praise God as a result of what I've learned this week?

How can I apply what I've learned this week to my life today and next week?

Where do I need His strength for today? Tomorrow? Next week?

Is there a verse from this week that I should commit to memory? Write it on the next page or on a 3x5 card to take with you to memorize.

Are there any sins I need to confess to God in prayer?

Is there anyone I need to forgive? Is there anyone I need to ask forgiveness of?

Are there any seeds of bitterness starting to take root in my heart?

Are there any fears or worries I need to lay at His feet?

notes, verses to memorize

prayers, doodles, etc

☐ pray before beginning

Leviticus 22

Date:

Summarize the main idea(s) in this chapter:

Verse(s) that stood out   or   Who is in this chapter? What do they say? What do they do?

Why did I pick this verse?   or   What is going on? Is there anything going wrong?

Definitions of words and/or cross references from my verse   or   When and where did this happen?

#Iwillmeditate

Rewrite the verse in your own words or personalize it.

or

Why is this chapter in the Bible?
Why did these events happen?
Why did the people act this way?

Does this verse reveal anything about God/Jesus/Holy Spirit?
Are there examples to follow or avoid? What does this chapter have to teach me?

How can I apply insights from this verse today? This week?

Notes, quotes, doodles, checklists, prayers, etc.

#Iwillmeditate

☐ pray before beginning

Leviticus 23

Date:

Summarize the main idea(s) in this chapter:

Verse(s) that stood out   or   **Who is in this chapter? What do they say? What do they do?**

Why did I pick this verse?   or   **What is going on? Is there anything going wrong?**

Definitions of words and/or cross references from my verse   or   **When and where did this happen?**

#Iwillmeditate

Rewrite the verse in your own words　　　or　　　Why is this chapter in the Bible?
or personalize it.　　　　　　　　　　　　　　　Why did these events happen?
　　　　　　　　　　　　　　　　　　　　　　　Why did the people act this way?

Does this verse reveal anything about God/Jesus/Holy Spirit?
Are there examples to follow or avoid? What does this chapter have to teach me?

How can I apply insights from this verse today? This week?

Notes, quotes, doodles, checklists, prayers, etc.

#Iwillmeditate

☐ pray before beginning

Leviticus 24

Date:

Summarize the main idea(s) in this chapter:

Verse(s) that stood out   or   **Who is in this chapter? What do they say? What do they do?**

Why did I pick this verse?   or   **What is going on? Is there anything going wrong?**

Definitions of words and/or cross references from my verse   or   **When and where did this happen?**

#Iwillmeditate

Rewrite the verse in your own words or personalize it.   or   Why is this chapter in the Bible? Why did these events happen? Why did the people act this way?

Does this verse reveal anything about God/Jesus/Holy Spirit? Are there examples to follow or avoid? What does this chapter have to teach me?

How can I apply insights from this verse today? This week?

Notes, quotes, doodles, checklists, prayers, etc.

☐ pray before beginning

Leviticus 25

Date:

Summarize the main idea(s) in this chapter:

Verse(s) that stood out or **Who is in this chapter? What do they say? What do they do?**

Why did I pick this verse? or **What is going on? Is there anything going wrong?**

Definitions of words and/or cross references from my verse or **When and where did this happen?**

#Iwillmeditate

Rewrite the verse in your own words or personalize it.

or

Why is this chapter in the Bible?
Why did these events happen?
Why did the people act this way?

Does this verse reveal anything about God/Jesus/Holy Spirit?
Are there examples to follow or avoid? What does this chapter have to teach me?

How can I apply insights from this verse today? This week?

Notes, quotes, doodles, checklists, prayers, etc.

#Iwillmeditate

☐ pray before beginning

Leviticus 26

Date:

Summarize the main idea(s) in this chapter:

Verse(s) that stood out or **Who is in this chapter? What do they say? What do they do?**

Why did I pick this verse? or **What is going on? Is there anything going wrong?**

Definitions of words and/or cross references from my verse or **When and where did this happen?**

#Iwillmeditate

Rewrite the verse in your own words or Why is this chapter in the Bible?
or personalize it. Why did these events happen?
 Why did the people act this way?

Does this verse reveal anything about God/Jesus/Holy Spirit?
Are there examples to follow or avoid? What does this chapter have to teach me?

How can I apply insights from this verse today? This week?

Notes, quotes, doodles, checklists, prayers, etc.

#Iwillmeditate

☐ pray before beginning

Leviticus 27

Date:

Summarize the main idea(s) in this chapter:

Verse(s) that stood out   or   **Who is in this chapter? What do they say? What do they do?**

Why did I pick this verse?   or   **What is going on? Is there anything going wrong?**

Definitions of words and/or cross references from my verse   or   **When and where did this happen?**

#Iwillmeditate

Rewrite the verse in your own words   or   Why is this chapter in the Bible?
or personalize it.   Why did these events happen?
                                                Why did the people act this way?

Does this verse reveal anything about God/Jesus/Holy Spirit?
Are there examples to follow or avoid? What does this chapter have to teach me?

How can I apply insights from this verse today? This week?

Notes, quotes, doodles, checklists, prayers, etc.

#Iwillmeditate

☐ pray before beginning

Review and reflect #24

Date:

Review each of the last six days work. Write or list the main takeaway you got from each chapter. (Look closely at the sections "What does this reveal about God?" and "How can I apply this?")

Are there any themes showing up in this week's work?

Are there any areas God is wanting to grow my faith or trust?
Are there any insights from this week's work on how to do this?

Are there any sins God is spotlighting in my life?
Are there any insights from this week's work on how to kill these sins?

#Iwillmeditate

Re-read one or two of the most impactful verses from this week and turn them into a prayer. (There is room on the next pages to write it down if you want.)

How can I thank or praise God as a result of what I've learned this week?

How can I apply what I've learned this week to my life today and next week?

Where do I need His strength for today? Tomorrow? Next week?

Is there a verse from this week that I should commit to memory? Write it on the next page or on a 3x5 card to take with you to memorize.

Are there any sins I need to confess to God in prayer?

Is there anyone I need to forgive? Is there anyone I need to ask forgiveness of?

Are there any seeds of bitterness starting to take root in my heart?

Are there any fears or worries I need to lay at His feet?

notes, verses to memorize

prayers, doodles, etc

☐ pray before beginning

Luke 1

Date:

Summarize the main idea(s) in this chapter:

Verse(s) that stood out or Who is in this chapter?
 What do they say? What do they do?

Why did I pick this verse? or What is going on?
 Is there anything going wrong?

Definitions of words and/or or When and where
cross references from my verse did this happen?

#Iwillmeditate

Rewrite the verse in your own words　　or　　Why is this chapter in the Bible?
or personalize it.　　　　　　　　　　　　Why did these events happen?
　　　　　　　　　　　　　　　　　　　　Why did the people act this way?

Does this verse reveal anything about God/Jesus/Holy Spirit?
Are there examples to follow or avoid? What does this chapter have to teach me?

How can I apply insights from this verse today? This week?

Notes, quotes, doodles, checklists, prayers, etc.

☐ pray before beginning

Luke 2

Date:

Summarize the main idea(s) in this chapter:

Verse(s) that stood out or **Who is in this chapter? What do they say? What do they do?**

Why did I pick this verse? or **What is going on? Is there anything going wrong?**

Definitions of words and/or cross references from my verse or **When and where did this happen?**

#Iwillmeditate

Rewrite the verse in your own words or personalize it. **or** Why is this chapter in the Bible? Why did these events happen? Why did the people act this way?

Does this verse reveal anything about God/Jesus/Holy Spirit? Are there examples to follow or avoid? What does this chapter have to teach me?

How can I apply insights from this verse today? This week?

Notes, quotes, doodles, checklists, prayers, etc.

#Iwillmeditate

☐ pray before beginning

Luke 3

Date:

Summarize the main idea(s) in this chapter:

Verse(s) that stood out   or   **Who is in this chapter? What do they say? What do they do?**

Why did I pick this verse?   or   **What is going on? Is there anything going wrong?**

Definitions of words and/or cross references from my verse   or   **When and where did this happen?**

#Iwillmeditate

Rewrite the verse in your own words　　or　　Why is this chapter in the Bible?
or personalize it.　　　　　　　　　　　　　　Why did these events happen?
　　　　　　　　　　　　　　　　　　　　　　Why did the people act this way?

Does this verse reveal anything about God/Jesus/Holy Spirit?
Are there examples to follow or avoid? What does this chapter have to teach me?

How can I apply insights from this verse today? This week?

Notes, quotes, doodles, checklists, prayers, etc.

#Iwillmeditate

☐ pray before beginning

Luke 4

Date:

Summarize the main idea(s) in this chapter:

Verse(s) that stood out   or   **Who is in this chapter? What do they say? What do they do?**

Why did I pick this verse?   or   **What is going on? Is there anything going wrong?**

Definitions of words and/or cross references from my verse   or   **When and where did this happen?**

#Iwillmeditate

Rewrite the verse in your own words or personalize it.   or   Why is this chapter in the Bible? Why did these events happen? Why did the people act this way?

Does this verse reveal anything about God/Jesus/Holy Spirit?
Are there examples to follow or avoid? What does this chapter have to teach me?

How can I apply insights from this verse today? This week?

Notes, quotes, doodles, checklists, prayers, etc.

#Iwillmeditate

☐ pray before beginning

Luke 5

Date:

Summarize the main idea(s) in this chapter:

Verse(s) that stood out   or   Who is in this chapter?
What do they say? What do they do?

Why did I pick this verse?   or   What is going on?
Is there anything going wrong?

Definitions of words and/or   or   When and where
cross references from my verse   did this happen?

#Iwillmeditate

Rewrite the verse in your own words or personalize it.   or   Why is this chapter in the Bible?
Why did these events happen?
Why did the people act this way?

Does this verse reveal anything about God/Jesus/Holy Spirit?
Are there examples to follow or avoid? What does this chapter have to teach me?

How can I apply insights from this verse today? This week?

Notes, quotes, doodles, checklists, prayers, etc.

#Iwillmeditate

☐ pray before beginning

Luke 6

Date:

Summarize the main idea(s) in this chapter:

Verse(s) that stood out or Who is in this chapter? What do they say? What do they do?

Why did I pick this verse? or What is going on? Is there anything going wrong?

Definitions of words and/or cross references from my verse or When and where did this happen?

#Iwillmeditate

Rewrite the verse in your own words   or   Why is this chapter in the Bible?
or personalize it.   Why did these events happen?
                                                                    Why did the people act this way?

Does this verse reveal anything about God/Jesus/Holy Spirit?
Are there examples to follow or avoid? What does this chapter have to teach me?

How can I apply insights from this verse today? This week?

Notes, quotes, doodles, checklists, prayers, etc.

#Iwillmeditate

☐ pray before beginning

Review and reflect #25

Date:

Review each of the last six days work. Write or list the main takeaway you got from each chapter. (Look closely at the sections "What does this reveal about God?" and "How can I apply this?")

Are there any themes showing up in this week's work?

Are there any areas God is wanting to grow my faith or trust?
Are there any insights from this week's work on how to do this?

Are there any sins God is spotlighting in my life?
Are there any insights from this week's work on how to kill these sins?

#Iwillmeditate

Re-read one or two of the most impactful verses from this week and turn them into a prayer. (There is room on the next pages to write it down if you want.)

How can I thank or praise God as a result of what I've learned this week?

How can I apply what I've learned this week to my life today and next week?

Where do I need His strength for today? Tomorrow? Next week?

Is there a verse from this week that I should commit to memory? Write it on the next page or on a 3x5 card to take with you to memorize.

Are there any sins I need to confess to God in prayer?

Is there anyone I need to forgive? Is there anyone I need to ask forgiveness of?

Are there any seeds of bitterness starting to take root in my heart?

Are there any fears or worries I need to lay at His feet?

notes, verses to memorize

prayers, doodles, etc

☐ pray before beginning

Luke 7

Date:

Summarize the main idea(s) in this chapter:

Verse(s) that stood out   or   **Who is in this chapter? What do they say? What do they do?**

Why did I pick this verse?   or   **What is going on? Is there anything going wrong?**

Definitions of words and/or cross references from my verse   or   **When and where did this happen?**

#Iwillmeditate

Rewrite the verse in your own words　　　or　　Why is this chapter in the Bible?
or personalize it.　　　　　　　　　　　　　　Why did these events happen?
　　　　　　　　　　　　　　　　　　　　　　Why did the people act this way?

Does this verse reveal anything about God/Jesus/Holy Spirit?
Are there examples to follow or avoid? What does this chapter have to teach me?

How can I apply insights from this verse today? This week?

Notes, quotes, doodles, checklists, prayers, etc.

#Iwillmeditate

☐ pray before beginning

Luke 8

Date:

Summarize the main idea(s) in this chapter:

Verse(s) that stood out   or   **Who is in this chapter? What do they say? What do they do?**

Why did I pick this verse?   or   **What is going on? Is there anything going wrong?**

Definitions of words and/or cross references from my verse   or   **When and where did this happen?**

#Iwillmeditate

Rewrite the verse in your own words or personalize it.   or   Why is this chapter in the Bible?
Why did these events happen?
Why did the people act this way?

Does this verse reveal anything about God/Jesus/Holy Spirit?
Are there examples to follow or avoid? What does this chapter have to teach me?

How can I apply insights from this verse today? This week?

Notes, quotes, doodles, checklists, prayers, etc.

☐ pray before beginning

Luke 9

Date:

Summarize the main idea(s) in this chapter:

Verse(s) that stood out | or | Who is in this chapter?
What do they say? What do they do?

Why did I pick this verse? | or | What is going on?
Is there anything going wrong?

Definitions of words and/or cross references from my verse | or | When and where did this happen?

#Iwillmeditate

Rewrite the verse in your own words or personalize it.   or   Why is this chapter in the Bible? Why did these events happen? Why did the people act this way?

Does this verse reveal anything about God/Jesus/Holy Spirit? Are there examples to follow or avoid? What does this chapter have to teach me?

How can I apply insights from this verse today? This week?

Notes, quotes, doodles, checklists, prayers, etc.

#Iwillmeditate

☐ pray before beginning

Luke 10

Date:

Summarize the main idea(s) in this chapter:

Verse(s) that stood out   or   **Who is in this chapter? What do they say? What do they do?**

Why did I pick this verse?   or   **What is going on? Is there anything going wrong?**

Definitions of words and/or cross references from my verse   or   **When and where did this happen?**

#Iwillmeditate

Rewrite the verse in your own words or personalize it.   or   Why is this chapter in the Bible?
Why did these events happen?
Why did the people act this way?

Does this verse reveal anything about God/Jesus/Holy Spirit?
Are there examples to follow or avoid? What does this chapter have to teach me?

How can I apply insights from this verse today? This week?

Notes, quotes, doodles, checklists, prayers, etc.

#Iwillmeditate

☐ pray before beginning

Luke 11

Date:

Summarize the main idea(s) in this chapter:

Verse(s) that stood out   or   **Who is in this chapter? What do they say? What do they do?**

Why did I pick this verse?   or   **What is going on? Is there anything going wrong?**

Definitions of words and/or cross references from my verse   or   **When and where did this happen?**

#Iwillmeditate

Rewrite the verse in your own words   or   Why is this chapter in the Bible?
or personalize it.   Why did these events happen?
                                                Why did the people act this way?

Does this verse reveal anything about God/Jesus/Holy Spirit?
Are there examples to follow or avoid? What does this chapter have to teach me?

How can I apply insights from this verse today? This week?

Notes, quotes, doodles, checklists, prayers, etc.

#Iwillmeditate

☐ pray before beginning

Luke 12

Date:

Summarize the main idea(s) in this chapter:

Verse(s) that stood out   or   Who is in this chapter?
What do they say? What do they do?

Why did I pick this verse?   or   What is going on?
Is there anything going wrong?

Definitions of words and/or cross references from my verse   or   When and where did this happen?

#Iwillmeditate

Rewrite the verse in your own words or personalize it.

or

Why is this chapter in the Bible?
Why did these events happen?
Why did the people act this way?

Does this verse reveal anything about God/Jesus/Holy Spirit?
Are there examples to follow or avoid? What does this chapter have to teach me?

How can I apply insights from this verse today? This week?

Notes, quotes, doodles, checklists, prayers, etc.

#Iwillmeditate

☐ pray before beginning

Review and reflect #26

Date:

Review each of the last six days work. Write or list the main takeaway you got from each chapter. (Look closely at the sections "What does this reveal about God?" and "How can I apply this?")

Are there any themes showing up in this week's work?

Are there any areas God is wanting to grow my faith or trust?
Are there any insights from this week's work on how to do this?

Are there any sins God is spotlighting in my life?
Are there any insights from this week's work on how to kill these sins?

#Iwillmeditate

Re-read one or two of the most impactful verses from this week and turn them into a prayer. (There is room on the next pages to write it down if you want.)

How can I thank or praise God as a result of what I've learned this week?

How can I apply what I've learned this week to my life today and next week?

Where do I need His strength for today? Tomorrow? Next week?

Is there a verse from this week that I should commit to memory? Write it on the next page or on a 3x5 card to take with you to memorize.

Are there any sins I need to confess to God in prayer?

Is there anyone I need to forgive? Is there anyone I need to ask forgiveness of?

Are there any seeds of bitterness starting to take root in my heart?

Are there any fears or worries I need to lay at His feet?

notes, verses to memorize

prayers, doodles, etc

☐ pray before beginning

Luke 13

Date:

Summarize the main idea(s) in this chapter:

Verse(s) that stood out or **Who is in this chapter? What do they say? What do they do?**

Why did I pick this verse? or **What is going on? Is there anything going wrong?**

Definitions of words and/or cross references from my verse or **When and where did this happen?**

#Iwillmeditate

Rewrite the verse in your own words or personalize it.   or   Why is this chapter in the Bible?
Why did these events happen?
Why did the people act this way?

Does this verse reveal anything about God/Jesus/Holy Spirit?
Are there examples to follow or avoid? What does this chapter have to teach me?

How can I apply insights from this verse today? This week?

Notes, quotes, doodles, checklists, prayers, etc.

#Iwillmeditate

☐ pray before beginning

Luke 14

Date:

Summarize the main idea(s) in this chapter:

Verse(s) that stood out   or   **Who is in this chapter? What do they say? What do they do?**

Why did I pick this verse?   or   **What is going on? Is there anything going wrong?**

Definitions of words and/or cross references from my verse   or   **When and where did this happen?**

#Iwillmeditate

Rewrite the verse in your own words   or   Why is this chapter in the Bible?
or personalize it.   Why did these events happen?
                                                                         Why did the people act this way?

Does this verse reveal anything about God/Jesus/Holy Spirit?
Are there examples to follow or avoid? What does this chapter have to teach me?

How can I apply insights from this verse today? This week?

Notes, quotes, doodles, checklists, prayers, etc.

#Iwillmeditate

☐ pray before beginning

Luke 15

Date:

Summarize the main idea(s) in this chapter:

Verse(s) that stood out or Who is in this chapter?
What do they say? What do they do?

Why did I pick this verse? or What is going on?
Is there anything going wrong?

Definitions of words and/or or When and where
cross references from my verse did this happen?

#Iwillmeditate

Rewrite the verse in your own words   or   Why is this chapter in the Bible?
or personalize it.   Why did these events happen?
                                                   Why did the people act this way?

Does this verse reveal anything about God/Jesus/Holy Spirit?
Are there examples to follow or avoid? What does this chapter have to teach me?

How can I apply insights from this verse today? This week?

Notes, quotes, doodles, checklists, prayers, etc.

☐ pray before beginning

Luke 16

Date:

Summarize the main idea(s) in this chapter:

Verse(s) that stood out or **Who is in this chapter? What do they say? What do they do?**

Why did I pick this verse? or **What is going on? Is there anything going wrong?**

Definitions of words and/or cross references from my verse or **When and where did this happen?**

#Iwillmeditate

Rewrite the verse in your own words or Why is this chapter in the Bible?
or personalize it. Why did these events happen?
 Why did the people act this way?

Does this verse reveal anything about God/Jesus/Holy Spirit?
Are there examples to follow or avoid? What does this chapter have to teach me?

How can I apply insights from this verse today? This week?

Notes, quotes, doodles, checklists, prayers, etc.

☐ pray before beginning

Luke 17

Date:

Summarize the main idea(s) in this chapter:

Verse(s) that stood out or Who is in this chapter? What do they say? What do they do?

Why did I pick this verse? or What is going on? Is there anything going wrong?

Definitions of words and/or cross references from my verse or When and where did this happen?

#Iwillmeditate

Rewrite the verse in your own words or personalize it.   or   Why is this chapter in the Bible?
Why did these events happen?
Why did the people act this way?

Does this verse reveal anything about God/Jesus/Holy Spirit?
Are there examples to follow or avoid? What does this chapter have to teach me?

How can I apply insights from this verse today? This week?

Notes, quotes, doodles, checklists, prayers, etc.

#Iwillmeditate

☐ pray before beginning

Luke 18

Date:

Summarize the main idea(s) in this chapter:

Verse(s) that stood out   or   **Who is in this chapter? What do they say? What do they do?**

Why did I pick this verse?   or   **What is going on? Is there anything going wrong?**

Definitions of words and/or cross references from my verse   or   **When and where did this happen?**

#Iwillmeditate

Rewrite the verse in your own words or personalize it.

or

Why is this chapter in the Bible?
Why did these events happen?
Why did the people act this way?

Does this verse reveal anything about God/Jesus/Holy Spirit?
Are there examples to follow or avoid? What does this chapter have to teach me?

How can I apply insights from this verse today? This week?

Notes, quotes, doodles, checklists, prayers, etc.

#Iwillmeditate

☐ pray before beginning

Review and reflect #27

Date:

Review each of the last six days work. Write or list the main takeaway you got from each chapter. (Look closely at the sections "What does this reveal about God?" and "How can I apply this?")

Are there any themes showing up in this week's work?

Are there any areas God is wanting to grow my faith or trust?
Are there any insights from this week's work on how to do this?

Are there any sins God is spotlighting in my life?
Are there any insights from this week's work on how to kill these sins?

#Iwillmeditate

Re-read one or two of the most impactful verses from this week and turn them into a prayer. (There is room on the next pages to write it down if you want.)

How can I thank or praise God as a result of what I've learned this week?

How can I apply what I've learned this week to my life today and next week?

Where do I need His strength for today? Tomorrow? Next week?

Is there a verse from this week that I should commit to memory? Write it on the next page or on a 3x5 card to take with you to memorize.

Are there any sins I need to confess to God in prayer?

Is there anyone I need to forgive? Is there anyone I need to ask forgiveness of?

Are there any seeds of bitterness starting to take root in my heart?

Are there any fears or worries I need to lay at His feet?

notes, verses to memorize

prayers, doodles, etc

☐ pray before beginning

Luke 19

Date:

Summarize the main idea(s) in this chapter:

Verse(s) that stood out   or   **Who is in this chapter? What do they say? What do they do?**

Why did I pick this verse?   or   **What is going on? Is there anything going wrong?**

Definitions of words and/or cross references from my verse   or   **When and where did this happen?**

#Iwillmeditate

Rewrite the verse in your own words or personalize it.   or   Why is this chapter in the Bible? Why did these events happen? Why did the people act this way?

Does this verse reveal anything about God/Jesus/Holy Spirit? Are there examples to follow or avoid? What does this chapter have to teach me?

How can I apply insights from this verse today? This week?

Notes, quotes, doodles, checklists, prayers, etc.

#Iwillmeditate

☐ pray before beginning

Luke 20

Date:

Summarize the main idea(s) in this chapter:

Verse(s) that stood out or Who is in this chapter?
 What do they say? What do they do?

Why did I pick this verse? or What is going on?
 Is there anything going wrong?

Definitions of words and/or or When and where
cross references from my verse did this happen?

#Iwillmeditate

Rewrite the verse in your own words　　or　　Why is this chapter in the Bible?
or personalize it.　　　　　　　　　　　　Why did these events happen?
　　　　　　　　　　　　　　　　　　　　Why did the people act this way?

Does this verse reveal anything about God/Jesus/Holy Spirit?
Are there examples to follow or avoid? What does this chapter have to teach me?

How can I apply insights from this verse today? This week?

Notes, quotes, doodles, checklists, prayers, etc.

#Iwillmeditate

☐ pray before beginning

Luke 21

Date:

Summarize the main idea(s) in this chapter:

Verse(s) that stood out   or   **Who is in this chapter? What do they say? What do they do?**

Why did I pick this verse?   or   **What is going on? Is there anything going wrong?**

Definitions of words and/or cross references from my verse   or   **When and where did this happen?**

#Iwillmeditate

Rewrite the verse in your own words or personalize it.

or

Why is this chapter in the Bible?
Why did these events happen?
Why did the people act this way?

Does this verse reveal anything about God/Jesus/Holy Spirit?
Are there examples to follow or avoid? What does this chapter have to teach me?

How can I apply insights from this verse today? This week?

Notes, quotes, doodles, checklists, prayers, etc.

#Iwillmeditate

☐ pray before beginning

Luke 22

Date:

Summarize the main idea(s) in this chapter:

Verse(s) that stood out   or   Who is in this chapter?
What do they say? What do they do?

Why did I pick this verse?   or   What is going on?
Is there anything going wrong?

Definitions of words and/or   or   When and where
cross references from my verse   did this happen?

#Iwillmeditate

Rewrite the verse in your own words or Why is this chapter in the Bible?
or personalize it. Why did these events happen?
Why did the people act this way?

Does this verse reveal anything about God/Jesus/Holy Spirit?
Are there examples to follow or avoid? What does this chapter have to teach me?

How can I apply insights from this verse today? This week?

Notes, quotes, doodles, checklists, prayers, etc.

#Iwillmeditate

☐ pray before beginning

Luke 23

Date:

Summarize the main idea(s) in this chapter:

Verse(s) that stood out   or   Who is in this chapter?
What do they say? What do they do?

Why did I pick this verse?   or   What is going on?
Is there anything going wrong?

Definitions of words and/or   or   When and where
cross references from my verse   did this happen?

#Iwillmeditate

Rewrite the verse in your own words or personalize it.

or

Why is this chapter in the Bible?
Why did these events happen?
Why did the people act this way?

Does this verse reveal anything about God/Jesus/Holy Spirit?
Are there examples to follow or avoid? What does this chapter have to teach me?

How can I apply insights from this verse today? This week?

Notes, quotes, doodles, checklists, prayers, etc.

#Iwillmeditate

☐ pray before beginning

Luke 24

Date:

Summarize the main idea(s) in this chapter:

Verse(s) that stood out   or   **Who is in this chapter? What do they say? What do they do?**

Why did I pick this verse?   or   **What is going on? Is there anything going wrong?**

Definitions of words and/or cross references from my verse   or   **When and where did this happen?**

#Iwillmeditate

Rewrite the verse in your own words or personalize it.   or   Why is this chapter in the Bible?
Why did these events happen?
Why did the people act this way?

Does this verse reveal anything about God/Jesus/Holy Spirit?
Are there examples to follow or avoid? What does this chapter have to teach me?

How can I apply insights from this verse today? This week?

Notes, quotes, doodles, checklists, prayers, etc.

#Iwillmeditate

☐ pray before beginning

Review and reflect #28

Date:

Review each of the last six days work. Write or list the main takeaway you got from each chapter. (Look closely at the sections "What does this reveal about God?" and "How can I apply this?")

Are there any themes showing up in this week's work?

Are there any areas God is wanting to grow my faith or trust?
Are there any insights from this week's work on how to do this?

Are there any sins God is spotlighting in my life?
Are there any insights from this week's work on how to kill these sins?

#Iwillmeditate

Re-read one or two of the most impactful verses from this week and turn them into a prayer. (There is room on the next pages to write it down if you want.)

How can I thank or praise God as a result of what I've learned this week?

How can I apply what I've learned this week to my life today and next week?

Where do I need His strength for today? Tomorrow? Next week?

Is there a verse from this week that I should commit to memory? Write it on the next page or on a 3x5 card to take with you to memorize.

Are there any sins I need to confess to God in prayer?

Is there anyone I need to forgive? Is there anyone I need to ask forgiveness of?

Are there any seeds of bitterness starting to take root in my heart?

Are there any fears or worries I need to lay at His feet?

notes, verses to memorize

prayers, doodles, etc

Congratulations!

You did it! Great job on finishing. Look for Volume Three on Amazon to continue your journey through the Bible!

Also be sure to check out the Journal and Doodle Bible studies on Amazon and on my website www.StoneSoupforFive.com. These inductive Bible studies work through a book of the Bible with built in meditation, questions, doodles, and much more.

Bible Studies

www.StoneSoupforFive.com

Made in the USA
Lexington, KY
18 February 2019